GOLF · FLEX

Paul Frediani

GOLF·FLEX™

10 Minutes a Day to Better Play

Hatherleigh Press
New York
A GETFITNOW.com Book

Hatherleigh Press/GETFITNOW.com Books
An Affiliate of W.W. Norton & Company, Inc.
5-22 46th Avenue, Suite 200
Long Island City, NY 11101
1-800-367-2550
Visit our website: www.getfitnow.com

Disclaimer:
Before beginning any exercise program consult your physician. The
author and publisher of this book and workout disclaim any liability,
personal or professional, resulting from the misapplication of any of the
training procedures described in this publication.

All GETFITNOW.com titles are available for bulk purchase, special
promotions, and premiums. For more information, please contact the
manager of our Special Sales Department at 1-800-367-2550.

Library of Congress Cataloging-in-Publication Data
Frediani, Paul, 1952–
  [Golf flex]
  Paul Frediani's golf flex: 10 minutes a day to better play.
    p. cm.
  "A Getfitnow.com book."
  ISBN 1-57826-031-0 (alk. paper)
  1. Golf—Training. 2. Stretching exercises. I. Title: Golf flex. II. Title.

  GV979.E9 F74 1999
  613.7'11—dc21   99-052718

Cover design by Lisa Fyfe
Text design and composition by DC Designs

Principle photography by Peter Field Peck
with Canon® cameras and lenses on Fuji® slide film
Printed in Canada on acid-free paper
10 9 8 7 6 5 4

Additional photography copyright of Digital Stock,
a division of Corbis Corporation.

Quotations from golf pros courtesy of www.PGA.com, the official web
site of The PGA of America.

Acknowledgements

A big thanks to:

Matt Bloom, for getting the ball rolling

Tracy Tumminello, for her patience, encouragement, and editing talent

Andrew Flach, and the great people at Getfitnow.com for all the good energy

Peter Field Peck, for his magnificent photography

and Renee Meier, my love and guardian angel.

A special thanks to the following leaders in the fitness industry who are my friends, educators, and motivators, without whose passion and support this would not be possible: Annette Lang, Dos Condon, Bob Esquerre, and Rocco Greco.

CONTENTS

Part I – **INTRODUCTION**   **1**

Part II – **THE IMPORTANCE OF GOLF FLEX:**
       WHY STRETCH?   **3**

    Stretching Myths
    Improving Your Flexibility

Part III – **FLEXOLOGY**   **10**

    Flexspots
    Mechanics of the Golf Swing

Part IV – **THE GOLF FLEX PROGRAM**   **15**

    The Stretches
    Seated Stretches
    Throughout the Day

Part V — **INJURY HOT SPOTS AND
PREVENTION** **59**
Injury Hot Spots
Golfer's Elbow and Hand Strengthening
Strengthening the Rotator Cuffs
Lower Back
Hips
Feet and Ankles

Part VI — **CONCLUSION** **85**

MEET THE AUTHOR **87**

GOLF·FLEX

Part I

INTRODUCTION

Hi and welcome to Golf Flex! You have just taken a positive step to improve your golf game. My name is Paul Frediani and I am a fitness advisor and personal trainer. I create and develop fitness and flexibility programs for everyone from weekend warriors to professional athletes, and the one thing that they have in common is that they all dislike stretching. Why? Because they find it time-consuming, boring, and too complex. Not anymore. Golf Flex is simple, quick, and enjoyable. Follow me and learn how flexibility will increase your power, help you avoid injuries, and keep you in the game.

Golf Flex is a ten-minute a day flexibility program designed for golfers of all levels and ages. Golf Flex is specifically designed to prepare and warm up the muscles used in golf. This is called sports specificity. In addition, I have designed functional stretching for golfers that can be performed during their everyday living activities. This functional stretching incorporated into everyday tasks is the essence of Golf Flex.

The key to developing flexibility is consistency—plain and simple. If you move your body in specific motions, it will respond over a period of time. I am sure you did not pick up your golf club the first time and have a great game. You developed the skill over time, creating muscle memory. You will not achieve better range of motion in your joints unless you stretch regularly.

Golf Flex was developed not only to prepare you in a systematic and easy-to-follow way for your pre-game warm-up, but also, very importantly, to help you find and create ways to add stretching to your life on a consistent basis. What more can you ask for than a program that is enjoyable and effective, yet not time-consuming?

Part II

THE IMPORTANCE OF GOLF FLEX: WHY STRETCH?

Aren't we all interested in maintaining independence in our lives through mobility? None of us want to be slaves to our injuries, which can become chronic, forcing us to give up our active lifestyle. With just a little effort and an awareness of our daily living habits, we can avoid most common golf injuries. Strong research indicates that 80% of lower back problems in golf are caused by poor alignment of the spine and pelvic girdle. These problems can be a direct result of inflexibility, weak muscles, and poor postural habits.

When we get older, we naturally lose flexibility as we become less active, and this increases the risk of injury to our joints, tendons, and muscles. A consistent stretching program will reduce soreness and increase power in your game.

BENEFITS OF STRETCHING

- Reduces risk of injury
- Increases range of motion
- Increases body awareness
- Improves circulation
- Reduces muscle tension
- Reduces soreness
- Relaxes and relieves stress

THE WRONG WAY TO STRETCH

Hey! Get out of the way! Watch out! How often have you almost been brained by a flying golf club, or by someone swinging golf clubs around to get warmed up? I can't think of a worse way to stretch. Your muscles are cold and your grip is not yet warmed up. And, it is a good way to invite injury to yourself and someone else.

THE SCIENCE OF GOLF FLEX

Power is force produced over a distance per unit of time. In golf, power is the result of a total body as a chainlink summation of coordinated movements. If any of these three elements can be increased—force exerted, speed (unit of time at the head of the club during the downswing), or range of motion (flexibility)—the result will be a longer drive.

STRETCHING MYTHS

🌑 Myth 1—It's too time-consuming. There's no way I can fit it in my busy schedule.

You do not need to take time out from your day to stretch. You can start a flexibility program before you even get out of bed, while working in the office, or even in the car.

🌑 Myth 2—Flexibility training is for professional athletes only. It is much too complex to do alone. I would have to hire a personal trainer and spend a fortune.

Golf Flex is as easy as one, two, three. Complex fitness programs just don't work. If you have read this far, you're smart enough to follow this program. Save your money to buy new clubs.

🌑 Myth 3—I will never be flexible.

You will never be flexible if you don't stretch. It may be true that you'll never do splits, but short of major injuries, you can significantly improve your range of motion. The aging process naturally shortens and tightens your muscles. Flexibility training can help reverse that process.

⊕ Myth 4—I don't need to stretch everyday. I just stretch well once a week before I play.

Stretching once a week will do this for you—absolutely nothing. To increase your range of motion or improve flexibility, you need to stretch ten minutes a day. Consistency is the key.

⊕ Myth 5—Stretching is so boring.

Think about adding 20 to 40 yards to your drive. Boring? I think not. Professional golfers are adding that much yardage to their game simply because they have discovered the indisputable benefits of stretching. Lack of flexibility can make your golf swing short and narrow, reducing distance on your drive. So think about that when you start to yawn. What can be more boring than sitting home tending to your injuries? Reduce flexibility and you will increase your potential for serious injury.

⊕ Myth 6—I am too old to stretch.

It's never too late to begin a flexibility program. There is no better time than right now! If you want to be successful, avoid injuries, and have the satisfaction of a better game, stretching is the key. What are you waiting for? There are people running marathons in their 70s and 80s. The great John Glenn is back in space. Let's get busy! Let's stay active! Just a few minutes a day and you will see how much more limber you feel after only a few weeks.

IMPROVING YOUR FLEXIBILITY

> "Spend 5 to 7 minutes stretching and mentally preparing how you want to play."
>
> — JOHN STACEY, PGA PRO

Stay with the Golf Flex program. Give yourself time to stretch daily and you will be amazed at how quickly your body will respond. Do not over-stretch or give up if you miss a day. After a while, stretching will become as natural a part of your day as brushing your teeth.

Try to be aware of activities that can hinder your progress. Some of the simplest everyday tasks can hurt you in the long run—sitting with your legs crossed, carrying a bag slung over your shoulder, working hunched over at your desk. You can improve your flexibility by removing negative postural behavior.

Water, water, water. We lose flexibility as we get older largely due to the lack of movement needed to transport fluids to our joints. Drinking plenty of water helps replenish these necessary fluids, keeping our muscles flexible. Try to avoid caffeine and alcohol, or at least increase your water intake after drinking these beverages to reduce dehydration.

Remember that you can be very flexible in your lower body while still having a very tight upper body. Tailor your Golf Flex program to address your body's individual flexibility needs.

Part III

FLEXOLOGY

FLEXSPOTS

> "The most important aspect of a good golf swing is the stretch of the muscles."
>
> — DAVID GLENZ, PGA PRO

The following areas of the body are important to an overall flexibility program for golfers. Golf Flex will address each of these areas and how they relate to your golf swing. The golf swing is a complex action using many muscle groups together in a synchronized chainlink movement.

The flexspots are the muscle groups that work together to give you a fluid swing. Spend a little more time stretching the areas that are particularly tight. It is important when you do the Golf Flex stretches to follow the program in the order it is designed.

Neck—During your address, you are constantly putting stress on your neck. Warm up by relaxing the neck and preparing it for the impact and rotation of the swing.

Upper Back and Shoulders—Increased flexibility in the upper back and shoulders will allow for greater rotation and range of motion in your backswing, resulting in more speed and power.

Upper Arms—Focusing on this area will help the rotation of your swing by giving you greater range of motion through your elbow joints and shoulders.

Lower Back and Trunk—Definitely the most crucial area to keep flexible and healthy, the lower back is the center of your power drive. Every time you bend over to pick up a ball, you are lifting half your body weight. This is the most commonly injured and strained area of PGA and amateur golfers. The golf swing relies heavily on back stabilization and movement.

Inner and Outer Hips—Want to generate power? You`ve got to turn your hips. This is true in almost all sports. It is said that Joe Louis, the great heavyweight boxing champion, would turn his hips so crisply when he punched that you could hear his trunks snap against his thigh. The hip stretch is also essential for hip weight transfer during your golf swing.

Hands and Wrists—Prepare and warm up your hands and wrists for impact. Stretching these areas will help you avoid the nagging injury golfer's elbow, and give you better control of your clubs. Wrists that are limber will keep you out of the timber, wrist that are tight destroy ball flight.

Hamstrings and Quadriceps—Not only will tight hamstrings and quadriceps fatigue and tighten your legs, it will also effect your lower back and hips, considerably shortening your swing.

Calves, Achilles Tendon, and Ankles—Walking 18 holes can easily fatigue and cramp your calves. Stretching before and after your game will help prepare your muscles for the task of walking the course, and eliminate soreness. Achilles tendonitis, a common golf injury, can quickly become chronic. It can best be avoided by frequently stretching these areas well.

MECHANICS OF THE GOLF SWING

Let's take a look at the mechanics of a golf swing and how improving your flexibility can create more power in your drive. The golf swing is a complex motion, requiring the use of many joints in your body. The more joints used in a movement, such as throwing a football, swinging a bat, or throwing a punch, the more power your body is able to deliver.

You begin the golf swing as you address the ball with your ankles and knees slightly flexed. The leg, butt, and back muscles are engaged. The abdominal muscles are tight to protect the lower back, and the neck is flexed forward.

The right hip initiates the backswing as you shift your weight to your right foot. Rotation begins with your knees and your left hip rotates forward. The right side of your waist turns your torso as your shoulder muscles pull the club back. The rotator cuffs stabilize the shoulder girdle, and your elbow and wrist joints are both flexed. This action is reversed during the downswing and follow through.

By increasing the range of motion in all your joints and surrounding muscles, and by increasing the strength in your abdominal muscles to deliver power to your legs, hips, and upper torso, you will be able to deliver more power to your strokes.

Part IV

The Golf Flex Program

THE STRETCHES

> "*A tight mind is a tight body.*"
>
> - Tom Sutter, PGA Pro

Stretching is not a competition. What you do not achieve today may come tomorrow. However, you will never know if you don`t stay on path. Often times, people that are naturally talented in a certain activity never achieve greatness because they quit at the first obstacle. Commitment is all it takes.

In this program, we will focus on two types of stretching—static and functional active. Static stretching requires simply holding a stretch for 10 to 20 seconds.

As the simplest and safest stretch, this is where we'll begin. As you become more acquainted with your body and its range of motion, you can use functional active stretching. This type of stretching involves actively moving into a stretch and holding it for three to five seconds, repeating the motion five times. This is a more advanced and athletic stretch involving a greater risk of injury. Never force or strain your muscles when you stretch.

Before we begin, let's keep in mind some simple points:

1. Always breathe.

2. Maintain good posture.

3. Never hold your breath.

4. Never bounce or jerk.

5. Consistency is the key.

6. Stay in touch with your body and focus on the muscles being stretched.

7. Never over-stretch.

8. Consult a doctor before beginning any flexibility program.

9. Smile and relax.

10. And remember, always breathe.

Did you know that tightness is often a sign of muscular weakness? Flexibility and strength training go hand in hand. Identify your weakness and improve your strength.

THE STRETCHES

1. YES AND NO

Nod your head "Yes" by bringing your chin to your chest, then back up to the neutral position. Start the "No" movement by facing forward, turning your head slowly to the left until your chin is over your left shoulder, then slowly to the right until your chin is over the right shoulder. Neck exercises should be done gently. Repeat this exercise eight times.

Muscles used: Neck muscles.

Result: Prepares and warms up the neck for shoulder rotation and the impact of hitting the ball.

Tip: Add half moon rolls, which are chin rolls from one shoulder to the chest to the other shoulder. Be careful not to extend the neck backward.

2. SHOULDER ROLLS

Lift your shoulders to your ears—forward, down, back, and up. Reverse directions, and repeat the motion eight times both ways.

Muscles used: Shoulder muscles.

Result: Warms up the shoulders and prepares the neck for the impact of the swing.

Tip: Great stretch to relieve neck and shoulder tension.

3. BACK SCRATCHERS

Reach one elbow up toward the ceiling and your hand behind your neck and toward the opposite shoulder. With the other hand, assist the stretch by gently pulling back on the elbow. Repeat eight times on both sides.

Muscles used: Backs of arms, shoulders, and back muscles.

Result: Improves backswing, downswing, impact, and follow through.

Tip: Bend at the waist to increase the stretch.

4. BACK STRETCHER

Keeping your shoulders down, stretch your right arm across your chest, and gently pull your right arm towards you with your left hand. You can add more intensity by turning your torso. Switch arms and repeat eight times on both sides.

Muscles used: Upper back, arms, and shoulder muscles.

Result: Improves backswing and follow through.

Tip: Keep your shoulders down and away from the ears.

5. TREE HUGGER

With your feet shoulder width apart, pretend you're wrapping your arms around a big tree. Keep your chin to your chest as you contract your stomach muscles. You will feel this stretch from your tailbone to the top of your head. Repeat ten times.

Muscles used: Full back and spine stretch.

Result: Helps backswing, downswing, and impact.

Tip: Be sure to keep your abdominal muscles tight.

6. ROOSTER CROWS

Interlace your fingers behind your back. Squeeze your shoulder blades together as you stick out your chest, pressing your hands backward. Look up toward the ceiling, contract your butt, and stretch the front of your shoulders and chest. You want to keep your chest open to achieve a greater range of motion in both your back and forward swings. Combine with the Tree Hugger stretch, and repeat ten times.

Muscles used: Chest, front of shoulders, and upper back muscles.

Result: Improves backswing and follow through.

Tip: A slight arch in the lower back will increase this stretch. When stretching, remember your ears and shoulders are mortal enemies. Keep your shoulders down!

7. BYE-BYES

With your arms out to the sides, bend your forearms up from the elbows 90 degrees with your palms facing forward. Then, rotate your forearms, pressing your palms down. Repeat eight times.

Muscles used: Rotator Cuffs.

Result: Benefits the backswing, downswing, impact, and follow through.

Tip: Keep your shoulders stable and only rotate the arms. Work smoothly and slowly.

8. EMPTY BOTTLES

This is another great shoulder warm-up. Keep your arms straight and point your thumbs toward the floor. Start with your hands near your thighs and lift them over your head, repeating eight times.

Muscles used: Rotator Cuffs.

Result: Improves backswing, downswing, impact, and follow through.

Tip: Keep shoulders down and back.

9. PEACH PICKERS

With your feet shoulder width apart and your knees slightly bent, keep your stomach tight as you reach one hand toward the ceiling and the other toward the floor. Stretch your waist and shoulders as you alternate hands. Repeat the motion eight times. Advanced—For a more intense stretch, reach further and bend more from the waist.

Muscles used: Waist and shoulder muscles.

Result: Improves backswing, downswing, and follow through.

Tip: Deepen your knees by bending and reaching laterally to increase your stretch.

10. WILLOW TREE

Cross your feet, interlace your fingers, and reach the palms of your hands toward the ceiling. Advanced—Bend from the torso from side to side four times. Switch feet position and repeat.

Muscles used: Forearms, arms, fingers, shoulders, waist, hips, and legs.

Result: Improves address, backswing, downswing, and prepares the upper body for impact with the ball.

Tip: Keep your abdominal muscles contracted and your butt tight.

11. WRIST ROLL WITH FINGER SPREADER

With your fingers loose, roll your wrists clockwise, then counter-clockwise five times. Advanced—Press the tips of your fingers together as you separate your palms, stretching your fingers apart.

Muscles used: Hand and wrist muscles.

Result: Helps address and prepares the hands and wrists for impact with the ball.

Tip: If needed, repeat during play to help alleviate post-game soreness.

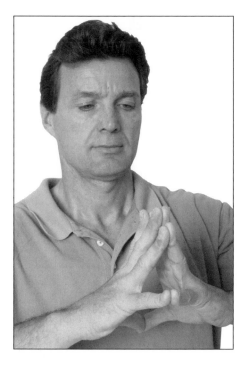

12. FOREARM FLEX AND STRETCH

With one arm extended in front of you, gently press
your fingers down with your opposite hand, palms
inward. Repeat the motion pulling your fingers back
with your palms facing outward. Perform this stretch
five times on each hand.

Muscles used: Forearm muscles.

Result: Improves
address and prepares the
forearms for impact with
the ball.

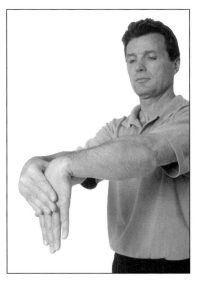

Tip: This stretch, in
combination with
strengthening exercises, will
help prevent Golfers' Elbow.

13. HELICOPTERS

Stand with your feet shoulder width apart and your arms extended out to the sides. Keep your face and hips forward as you rotate your torso to the left and right, keeping your arms straight. Advanced—Twist your torso as you reach your right hand to your left pocket and your left hand to your right pocket. This stretch is excellent for torso rotation. Switch sides and repeat ten times.

Muscles used: Waist and torso muscles.

Result: Improves your backswing, downswing, and follow through.

Tip: Start slowly and keep your face forward, increasing your rotation as you progress. Be sure your abdominal muscles are tight and your knees bent.

14. HULA HOOPS

Don't laugh, this is a great way to warm up through the hips. Think it's easy? Well, it was when you were twelve years old. With your hands on your hips, rotate your pelvis in circles. Repeat ten times in each direction.

Muscles used: Hips and waist muscles.

Result: Helps backswing, downswing, and follow through.

Tip: Start with small circles and gradually increase their size.

15. HAMSTRINGS

Bend forward at the waist, keeping your stomach tight and your back flat. Do not bounce. Stay where you can feel the stretch and hold for 10 seconds, repeating twice. Tight hamstrings = tight back = tight swing.

Muscles used: Back of leg muscles.

Result: Improves address, backswing, downswing, impact, and follow through and makes walking those 18 holes a little easier.

Tip: It is not how far you go, but how consistent you are with the stretches that will improve your flexibility.

16. QUADRICEPS

Standing straight, grab your foot or ankle behind you and pull your heel to your butt. Try to keep your knees together. Hold onto a chair or wall if you need additional support. Hold for 10 seconds, and repeat twice with each leg.

Muscles used: Quadricep muscles.

Result: Helps address, backswing, downswing, impact, and follow through.

Tip: By pressing your hips forward, you will increase the stretch in the front of your hips.

17. CALVES AND ACHILLES TENDONS

Walking 18 holes can easily fatigue your lower legs.
Standing with one foot in front of the other, keep your
feet facing forward and press your rear heel on the
ground. Feel the stretch in your calves for 10 seconds,
repeating twice. Advanced—Slightly bend your rear knee
for an advanced Achilles tendon stretch.

Muscles used: Calf muscles and Achilles tendons.

Result: Improves follow through, prevents Achilles
tendonitis, and prepares your calves for impact and
walking the course.

Tip: Be careful not to bounce when doing this stretch.

18. KNEE AND ANKLE ROTATORS

Place your hands on your knees and slightly bend your legs. Keep your knees and feet together as you rotate your knees clockwise and counter-clockwise eight times.

Muscles used: Knee and ankle muscles.

Result: Address, backswing, downswing, impact, and follow through are improved.

Tip:

Preparation is crucial for this area. The downswing puts a lot of stress on the knee joints. Start with small circles and work toward larger ones.

19. INNER THIGH

Stand with your feet more than shoulder width apart and rest your hands on your hips or thighs for support. Keep one leg straight while bending the other leg and hold for eight seconds. Switch legs and repeat four times. Advanced—For a more challenging stretch, place your hands on the floor between your legs.

Muscles used: Inner thigh muscles.

Result: Helps backswing and downswing, and prepares the leg muscles for impact with the ball.

Tip: If this stretch is too difficult, try the seated butterfly stretch (see page 44).

20. HAY BALERS

With your feet shoulder width apart and your palms together, stretch your arms straight out in front of you. Drop your hands to your left foot and then up over your right shoulder. Switch sides and repeat ten times.

Muscles used: Lower and upper legs, butt, waist, torso, shoulders, and arms.

Result: Improves address, backswing, downswing, impact, and follow through.

Tip: Hay balers are the final touch to complete our warm-up, combining all the stretches in a synchronized movement. Add one to three pound weights on each hand to increase the intensity of this exercise.

SEATED STRETCHES

These stretches are a wonderful addition to your Golf Flex workout and an excellent way to stretch in your spare time. The following stretches can be done while lying in bed or watching television, to help stretch your back and hips—two key power areas in golf.

Although these stretches may not be possible to do on the green, you should find time to practice them during the day.

21. INDIAN SITS

This is a great outer hip stretch. Start by sitting on the floor with your legs crossed, leaving both feet on the ground. Incorporate a back stretch by placing your hands on the floor in front of you. Lower your chin as you walk your hands forward, letting your chest fall to your knees. This is a wonderful multi-purpose exercise, which stretches your hips, butt, shoulders, and back. Alternate sides and repeat. Advanced—Increase your hip stretch by sitting with one foot over of the opposite knee.

22. CHILD POSE

Sit on your heels, drop your chest to your knees, and reach your hands out in front of you. A great relaxing stretch, this exercise stretches your ankles, legs, butt, and back.

23. BUTTERFLY

Sit with the soles of your feet together and your knees out to the sides. Hold your ankles as you gently press your knees apart with your elbows. Be careful not to bounce.

24. CORKSCREWS

Sit with your left leg straight and cross your right foot over your left leg. It is important to keep your back straight. Do not slouch! Place your right hand behind you, and your left arm outside your right leg. Turn and look toward your right hand. Be sure to pay attention to your breathing. Without changing feet position, turn and face the other direction. Hold each of these positions for 30 seconds. Repeat with the opposite leg.

25. ABDOMINAL AND BACK STRETCH

Lie on your stomach and lift your chest up on your elbows. Flex your abdominal muscles as you stretch your back. Advanced—Lift your entire upper body up on your hands. This is a much more intense stretch. It is not recommended for those recovering from lower back injuries.

26. LOWER BACK STRETCH

Lie on your back and bend one knee, while keeping the other leg straight. Hold the shin of your bent knee to your chest. Repeat with the opposite leg. Advanced—For added intensity, hold both shins to your chest.

27. TINKERBELL

Lying on your back, bend your right knee over the left, keeping your left leg straight. Pull the right leg across with your left hand and look in the opposite direction of the stretch. Reach your right hand out to the side and repeat with the opposite leg. Advanced—Keep your right leg straight as you cross it over your left leg. Hold both arms out to the sides. Repeat with the opposite leg.

POST GAME FLEX

While pre-game stretching warms your muscles, helps avoid injuries, and prepares your body for the movements of golf, post-game stretching alleviates soreness and keeps your muscles from snapping back tighter than they were before the game.

THROUGHOUT THE DAY

> "The most important thing is flexibility Find a good stretching routine and stick to it daily."
>
> -CAMERON DOAN, PGA PRO

The Golf Flex program is great, but how am I going to stretch during the week? I hardly have time to eat breakfast and kiss the family goodbye. I just don't have time for a flexibility program. This is the beauty of Golf Flex. You can practice your flexibility routine anywhere—at home, in the car, or at the office. Just do a few minutes at a time and you will achieve long-term results.

Now let's incorporate these stretches into our daily lives. You will see how easy it is to stretch as you do your everyday tasks, and how quickly your flexibility will increase.

In Bed. Do these stretches before you get out of bed in the morning and your back will love you.

Bring one knee to your chest, hold for 10 seconds, and alternate knees. Then, bring both knees to your chest for 10 seconds. Fold your knees over to one side, then the other side, holding for 10 seconds each. Be sure to keep your shoulders flat on the bed. As you increase in flexibility, move smoothly from one position to the next. These stretches will warm up, stretch, and prepare your back and spine for the day!

Rise and shine. Give yourself a big hug, stretching your upper and mid back. Hold one arm across your chest and hug it toward you with the opposite hand. Alternate arms, stretching the shoulder muscles.

From either a seated or standing position,

interlace your fingers and lift your hands over your head, pushing your palms away from you. This stretches your forearms, shoulders, and ribcage. This exercise can be increased by gently

leaning over to one side, stretching your waist. Be sure
to keep your abdominal muscles tight while doing this
stretch.

Time to shower. A nice hot
shower is an excellent
opportunity to warm up and
stretch. Start by letting the hot
water hit the back of your neck,
relaxing your upper back and
neck muscles. Slowly do half
circles, letting your chin roll from
one shoulder to the other. Repeat approximately six
times.

Now that your back is warmed up, do a few tree
huggers. Let the water run down your upper and mid
back. Hold each stretch for 10 seconds. Continue to
stretch your back by adding a few back scratchers.

Turn and face the water, letting it warm your chest
muscles as you do six rooster crows. You have just gotten
a great upper body stretch in no time. Shower everyday,
stretch everyday—see the
difference it makes!

Toweling off. Grab a towel at
both ends, bringing one hand over
your head and one behind your
back. Reverse the motion and
rotate your hands. This is a
wonderful way to stretch your

rotator cuffs and keep your shoulders healthy.

Stand with one foot forward, bending your rear knee and keeping your front leg straight while you towel off. To increase this stretch, wrap the towel around your forward foot and gently pull towards you. This exercise increases the strength and flexibility of your calves and Achilles tendons.

Reading the paper. You do it every morning! Take this time to also strengthen your hands and forearms. After reading a section of the paper, take a sheet in one hand and slowly crumble it into a tight ball. This is a lot harder than it seems. Try getting up to four sheets per hand.

Getting dressed. Putting on a T-shirt is something we do everyday and it can be a great stretch for our shoulders, ribcage, and arms. As you put one arm through your shirt, reach as far as you can toward the sky, and repeat with the opposite arm.

Putting on socks and shoes.

While seated, cross one ankle over the opposite knee and feel the stretch in the back of your legs and butt as you lean over to put on your sock. Reverse leg position and put on the other sock. Then slip on your shoes. Go down on one knee as you tie

your shoe, stretching the front of your hip and your back leg.

Sitting in the car,

waiting for it to warm up. Keep your right hand on the steering wheel and reach your left hand across your

body to the back of your seat. This really opens up your back and shoulders. Repeat on the opposite side.

Interlace both hands behind your head and reach backward, stretching both your chest and back.

At the office. For many, sitting at the office all day can make us tight and often tense. Sitting with our legs crossed for hours at a time while hunched over our desks, does nothing to promote flexibility. However, taking just a few minutes a day, you can easily increase your well-being and flexibility. There is an old Italian saying, "Chi va piano va sano e lontano," meaning, " He who goes slow, goes safely and far." A little every day will get you results!

Sit with your left ankle over your right knee. Keeping your spine straight, place your right hand on your left knee, and turn your torso to your left. In the same seated position, turn your torso to the right by placing your left hand on the outside of your right thigh. This is a great spine stretch! Continue by placing both hands on your thighs and gently lower your chest toward your knees, stretching your butt, back, and thighs. Reverse feet position and repeat.

Sit with your feet flat on the floor and slowly drop your head between your knees, letting your hands fall to the floor. You will feel this stretch in your lower back and butt. While in this stretch position, remember to breathe deeply into your lower back, filling your lungs and slowly letting tension release with each exhale.

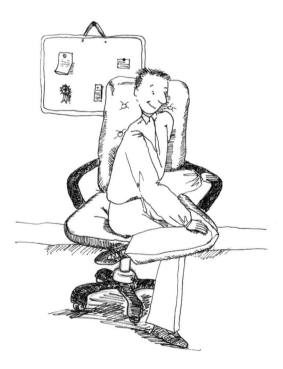

Grab both sides of the doorway with your hands at shoulder level. Walk forward until you feel the stretch in your arms. This exercise is great for your chest and shoulder muscles.

The following stretches can also be done seated at your desk:

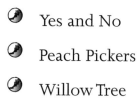

Yes and No

Peach Pickers

Willow Tree

Part V

Golf Flex Injury Hot Spots and Prevention

While muscle overuse is a common cause of injury for professional golfers, weekend golfers' injuries are most often a result of improper form, muscle weakness, and lack of flexibility.

You will notice the back, abs, and hips are included in the following injury prevention exercises. These areas are sometimes referred to as the power zone. In any sport that requires the motion of throwing or swinging, this part of the body stabilizes and generates power from your trunk to your torso.

INJURY HOT SPOTS

Elbows/Wrists/Forearms—Gripping the club often results in impact and overuse injuries.

Shoulders—The shoulders are the most common area injured in any sport that involves throwing or swinging.

Back—The golf swing can cause major strain from the neck to the lower back.

Hips—If your hips are tight, you will not generate rotation power; and if your back is tight, your hips will overcompensate, causing overuse injuries.

Feet/Ankles—Walking 18 holes can cause soreness in the front of your ankle and the soles of your feet, and also may result in shin splints.

GOLFER'S ELBOW AND HAND STRENGTHENING

> *"We need our wrists and forearms to be flexible."*
>
> -JOHN BUCZEK, PGA PRO

Golfer's elbow is a nagging, painful injury that, if not properly cared for, can become chronic. A form of tendonitis, golfer's elbow is a result of wear and tear over time. To care for this injury, there is one word you should burn into your memory—RICE. No, not the kind you get with Kung Pao chicken. R.I.C.E. is an acronym for:

Rest—to prevent further injury and relieve stress from the area of discomfort.

Ice—reduce swelling by decreasing circulation to the area.

Compression—bracing or wrapping the injured area to reduce expanding and swelling.

Elevation—to decrease the amount of blood and fluid to the irritated area.

Depending on its severity, golfer's elbow can take six weeks or longer to heal. It is important to see a doctor for a proper diagnosis. Once the inflammation is reduced, you can incorporate stretching and strengthening exercises. The biggest mistake most people make is not resting long enough. Coming back too soon can result in re-injury and further damage. The key to recovery is REST.

Wouldn't it be even smarter to avoid this injury instead of rehabilitating it? Let's look at some simple and effective stretching and strengthening exercises.

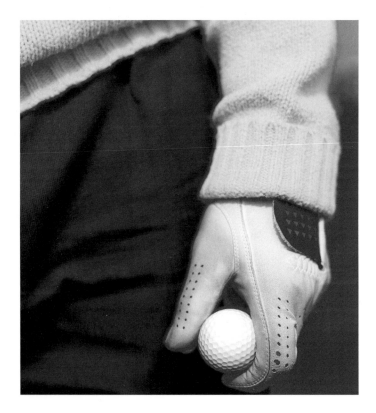

Hand Squeeze — Spread open your hand, then make a tight fist. Continue to open and close your hands, working up to 50 times.

Hand Squeeze With Resistance — Using a pliable rubber ball or old tennis ball, squeeze and release your fist. Keep a ball handy at your desk and do this exercise throughout the day.

Sand Gripping — Fill a bucket with sand and shove your hand in up to your wrist. Keep your hand in the sand as you open and close your fist. This is one tough exercise, but it will give you great results!

Let's begin where the tires hit the road—the hands, wrists, and forearms. Any weakness here will surely result in golfer's elbow. Strengthening the hands will give you the control needed to improve your game and avoid injury.

As mentioned earlier, a simple way to incorporate hand strengthening exercises into your day can be done while reading the newspaper. Taking one sheet at a time, use one hand to crumple the page into a tight ball. Do three or four sheets a day and you will notice an increased hand grip. When you swing, your wrists and hands work to generate power and control the golf club.

STRENGTHENING THE ROTATOR CUFFS

One of the most complex joints in the body, most of us
are not even sure what rotator cuffs are. The rotators,
commonly called rotator cuffs, are four little muscles
that stabilize your arms and shoulders during your golf
swing. Many golfers suffer from shoulder injuries due to
weak or strained rotator cuffs. If you want to stay in the
game, it is crucial to maintain healthy rotators. Here are
four simple stretching and strengthening exercises to
keep your rotator cuffs and shoulders happy and healthy.

Tips

1. Always stretch after performing these
   exercises.

2. Use a pillow or rolled up towel to support
   your head if you feel neck strain.

3. Work in slow and controlled movements.

4. Use a full range of motion.

1. BYE-BYES

With your arms out to the sides, bend your forearms up from the elbows 90 degrees with your palms facing forward. Then, rotate your forearms, pressing your palms down. Repeat eight times. Keep your shoulders stable and only rotate your arms. Work smoothly and slowly.

2. SOUP CANS

Use the same movement as the Empty Bottles stretch described on page 26, but add resistance. Do three sets of 10, starting with soup cans and working up to three-pound weights. Keep your arms straight and point your thumbs toward the floor, with your pinkies up toward the ceiling. Start with your hands near your thighs and lift them at a 45-degree angle over your head, repeating eight times.

3. EXTERNAL ROTATIONS

Lie on your side with your legs together and your knees bent. Place your bottom arm behind your head for support and your top arm at your waist, bent 90 degrees. Rotate your forearm from your stomach straight up and repeat on the other side. Start with three sets of 20, using one- to three-pound weights and work up to five pounds.

4. INTERNAL ROTATIONS

Lie on your side with your legs together and your knees bent. Rest on your shoulder with your top arm at your hip, and your bottom arm bent 90 degrees. Rotate your bottom arm from your stomach to the floor and repeat on the other side. Start with three sets of 20 using one- to three-pound weights and work up to five pounds.

LOWER BACK

> "Eight percent of all golfers will incur some sort of back pain during their golf careers."
>
> —Dr. Jim Suttie, PGA M.D.

The back takes on such a tremendous amount of stress during the golf swing that it is no wonder the lower back is a major source of injury for golfers. Before engaging in a back strengthening and stretching program, it is important to consult your doctor. The back is a complex area. Problems can arise from stress, poor posture, and certainly poor mechanics of the golf swing.

To maintain and condition your lower back, it is essential to keep it strong and flexible. The following are back strengthening exercises. They should be done in conjunction with abdominal exercises. Strengthening your abdominal muscles is an essential part of maintaining an overall healthy and strong back. The abdominal muscles help stabilize the back, while the obliques rotate your torso during your swing. No back conditioning program is complete without abdominal exercises.

BACK EXERCISES

1. SUPERMAN

Lie on your stomach and extend your arms in front of you. Lift your chest and arms off the ground.

2. LOIS LANE

Lie on your stomach with your hands under your chin.
Keep your chest on the floor as you lift your thighs and
feet.

3. SWIMMER

In the same position as the superman stretch, lift your right arm and left leg. Repeat with the opposite arm and leg.

Tip

Holding your knees to your chest is a great way to give your back an overall stretch after exercising.

Seated stretches that add flexibility to your back:

1. Indian Sits

2. Child Pose

3. Butterfly

4. Corkscrews

5. Abdominal and Back Stretch

6. Lower Back Stretch

7. Tinkerbell

ABDOMINAL EXERCISES

1. STANDARD CRUNCH

Lie on your back with your knees bent. With your hands behind your head, contract your abdominal muscles and lift your shoulders off the floor. Be careful not to pull on your neck.

2. OBLIQUE CRUNCHES

Lie on your back with your knees together to one side, and lift your shoulders off the floor. Repeat on both sides.

Tip:

Keeping your elbows flat, not pointed, reduces the strain on your neck.

3. REVERSE CURLS

Lie on your back with your knees and feet in the air, and place your hands on the floor at your sides. Lift your hips off the ground and tilt your pelvis up toward your chest. Do not bounce or jerk. Cross your feet for additional comfort. Advanced—With your hands behind your head, lift your hips, shoulders, and head.

HIPS

"Good hip rotation promotes a good swing."

-LINDA MULHERIN, PGA PRO

The most important part of the power zone, strong and flexible hips will keep you in the game and prevent nagging strains. Fortunately, we have many opportunities throughout the day to stretch our hips. Putting on your socks is a great way to work the sides of your hips, lacing your shoes works the front, and bending over while seated at your desk works the inner thighs.

Here are a few simple thigh and hip strengthening exercises:

1. SCISSORS

Lie on your side with your legs straight, and lift your top leg away from your bottom leg. Repeat on both sides.

2. INNER THIGH

On your side, cross one foot over the other leg and lift the straight leg six inches off the ground. Repeat on both sides.

3. STANDING SQUATS

Stand with your feet shoulder width apart. Cross your arms against your chest and keep your heels solid on the ground. Drop your butt back as though you were sitting in a chair. Keep your chest high and shoulders back as you try to keep your butt level with your knees.

FEET AND ANKLES

You can't play golf if you're not on your feet. The feet are your base of balance and power. Try throwing a baseball sitting in a chair.

A quick calves and Achilles stretch helps to prepare your calf muscles and Achilles tendons for walking 18 holes. Stretch the front of your ankles by sitting on the heel of your foot on the floor. Do the same stretch standing as you gently roll your foot forward. You can even do this stretch while on the course. A great way to massage aching feet and prevent plantar fasciitis, or heel spurs, is to stretch after a game. Your feet will love you for it!

Part VI

CONCLUSION

A FINAL NOTE

Golf Flex was developed out of necessity. As my golfing clients rolled in on monday mornings complaining of muscle weakness and soreness after playing a couple of rounds of golf on the weekend, I encouraged them to stretch before and after every game.

The response I always got was, "Of course I stretch. Everyone stretches before the game. That's nothing new. Everyone knows the benefits of flexibility training and how it improves your game." So, if they were stretching, why were they always so banged up and sore? So I asked them how they stretched. The response was always the same. "Oh well, I . . . uh, you know, uh, . . . do some of these and then I swing the club around, and . . . uh, you know, loosen up."

It was pretty obvious that they didn't have a handle on what they were doing, and that they probably picked up most of what they did from what they saw other golfers doing on the course. Golfers know golf, not stretching. It was apparent they had no systematic approach to stretching that they could follow in a safe and effective way.

I developed Golf Flex so golfers could understand and perform stretches in a simple and clear manner. It is just as important for golfers to continue their stretching everyday to increase flexibility and range of motion in a progressive matter. Golf Flex not only improves your golf game, but also leads to increased body awareness and well-being. You can achieve results, so what are you waiting for? When it comes to stretching, there's never an excuse not to do something.

In health and fitness,
Paul Frediani

MEET THE AUTHOR

An educator for the American Council of Exercise, Paul's interest in fitness began when he was twelve years old, surfing the chilly waters in San Francisco. His interest in sports and fitness led him to compete in open ocean swims, long distance running, and triathlons. He won the San Francisco Golden Gloves and the Pacific Coast Diamond Belt Light-Heavy Weight Boxing Championships. Paul is certified by the American Exercise College of Sports Medicine and is a medical exercise specialist. He is affiliated with Equinox Gyms in New York City, a fitness advisor for Getfitnow.com, and President of BoxAthletics, a fitness training company.

Crunch® Fitness Series

Through the country Crunch® is synonymous with the ultimate in fitness and exercise. From New York to LA, Crunch Fitness Centers have helped hundreds of thousands of Americans get in shape and stay in shape. With their unique lifestyle approach to fitness and their philosophy of "no judgements" on your lifestyle, Crunch is the choice of men and women who want to exercise their right to fitness.

Crunch and Hatherleigh are proud to announce the next three books in the *Crunch Fitness Series*. Each book in the series is specifically designed to meet the lifestyle demands of today's Americans — the harried business executive who spends her weekends on the road, the father of the bride who has to look good in a tux, the soccer mom who just doesn't have time for the gym, young people, old people, couch potatoes and bodybuilders.

Everyone will benefit from the Crunch expertise and their team of fitness specialists.

Crunch is a major national chain of fitness centers. Their brand is widely recognized through a daily television exercise show on ESPN and through their videos and fitness apparel. Their upscale, user-friendly gyms are located in New York, Los Angeles, San Francisco, Miami, Chicago, and Tokyo.

Also available in the
Crunch Fitness Series:

Beginner's Luck
Get Fit in a
Crunch
The Road
Warrior Workout

Perfect Posture
Mom always told you to stand up straight, and she was right!

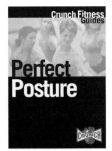

Good posture is very beneficial in a variety of ways — it can make you look better, feel better, and helps relieve a wide range of muscle and spine related complaints. The Crunch Perfect Posture book presents a combination of exercises, stretches and "Americanized" yoga techniques that will lead you to improved posture.

Also included are tips on selecting a mattress, the proper way to sit, how to prevent back injuries, and breathing exercises to help your spine and back.

October 1999 / $14.95 (Can. $20.99) / paper / 120 pages
ISBN 1-57826-040-X / 6 x 9   Diet & Health/Fitness

Workouts for Workaholics
Get your body in shape while you keep you career in gear!

Maintaining fitness on the job will help you work more productively, deal better with physical and emotional stress, and reduce sickness. This book shows you how to find the time at work to keep in shape. Includes exercises that can be done at your desk in business attire, relaxation techniques to fight stress, nutrition tips, and scheduling plans to get you out of the workplace and to a workout with the last amount of disruption.

October 1999 / $14.95 (Can. $20.99) / paper / 120 pages
ISBN 1-57826-041-8 / 6 x 9   Diet & Health/Fitness

On Your Mark. Get Set. Go!
Training for you first marathon.

The marathon is the crown jewel of running. 26.2 miles of exhilaration and sometimes agony. This book is designed to get the novice, recreational runner from the starting line to the finish line. In keeping with Crunch's philosophy, there's no judgement on your finishing time, we just want you to finish. Covers everything to get you in shape mentally and physically including nutrition, detailed training schedules, exercises and stretches, the right equipment, dealing with pain and avoiding injuries.

October 1999 / $14.95 (Can. $20.99) / paper / 120 pages
ISBN 1-57826-050-7 / 6 x 9   Diet & Health/Fitness

www.getfitnow.com

Golf Flex Video

Coming Soon!

Two New Titles in the *Sports Flex™* Series

Flexibility and conditioning for the amateur athlete

Net Flex™

A simple, easy-to-follow stretching program to improve your tennis game. Scientifically designed to stretch the muscles used in tennis, *Net Flex* will benefit players at all levels, from beginners to regular weekend players to the top tournament seeds. These simple stretching exercises can be done almost anywhere – in your office, at the clubhouse, at home or on the court.

April 2000 $9.95 paperback   ISBN 1-57826-077-9

Surf Flex™

Hey dude, wanna get tubular? Try the simple, user-friendly stretching exercises in *Surf Flex* before you hit the waves. Perhaps no other sport requires more agility and flexibility than surfing. Wiping out is no fun and flexibility will help prevent injuries. So before your try to hang ten, try the exercises in *Surf Flex*. It's guaranteed to keep your Wednesday's big and your summer's endless.

April 2000 $9.95 paperback   ISBN 1-57826-078-7

Author
Paul Frediani is a nationally recognized fitness trainer and educator. He is certified by the American College of Sports Medicine as a Medical Exercise Specialist and by the American Council on Exercise. He is affiliated with the Equinox Health Club in New York, and is president of BoxAthletics, a fitness training company.

I Can't Believe It's Yoga!

It's Yoga — American Style

Lisa Trivell, Photographed by
Peter Field Peck

A popular form of exercise and fitness conditioning, yoga combines stretching and breathing to tone the body, relax the muscles, and relieve tension. The numerous benefits of yoga can easily be added to anyone's daily fitness routine.

For many, though, yoga is seen as being both too difficult and too different to try. *I Can't Believe It's Yoga* addresses this perception problem by presenting a yoga based fitness program which is easy to accomplish.

In *I Can't Believe It's Yoga*, Lisa Trivell, an experienced yoga instructor transforms even the reluctant skeptic into an avid fan. Utilizing the most basic yoga exercises, the results are incredible!

IBSN 1-57826-032-9 / $14.95

Available in bookstores everywhere, order toll free at 1-800-906-1234 or online at getfitnow.com.